home living workbooks

bed linens

home living workbooks

bed linens

Katrin Cargill

photography by **James Merrell**

Clarkson Potter/Publishers
New York

Text copyright © 1998 by Katrin Cargill
Design copyright © 1998 by Ryland Peters & Small

Published by Clarkson N. Potter, Inc.,
201 East 50th Street, New York, New York 10022.
Member of the Crown Publishing Group.
Originally published in Great Britain by Ryland
Peters & Small in 1998.

Random House, Inc. New York, Toronto, London,
Sydney, Auckland.
http://www.randomhouse.com/

CLARKSON N. POTTER, POTTER, and colophon
are trademarks of Clarkson N. Potter, Inc.

Printed in China

Library of Congress Cataloging-in-Publication Data
is available upon request

ISBN 0-609-60126-1

10 9 8 7 6 5 4 3 2 1

First American Edition

contents

considering we spend a large portion of our lives in bed, we
owe it to ourselves to make our beds and bedrooms as comfortable and
relaxing as we can. In the course of working on this book, I have seen a lot
of bedrooms, some of them calm havens for relaxation and romance and
others welcoming spaces conducive to unwinding from the stresses of
everyday life. However, all too often, the bedroom is simply a basic space
for sleep, its only adornment a rumpled comforter unceremoniously thrown
over the bed. Whatever happened to the slightly self-indulgent luxury of
slipping between cool cotton sheets beneath a cozy woolen blanket, curling
up under a snug quilt for an afternoon nap, or sipping an early-morning
cup of coffee propped up against a comfortable padded headboard?

If we are relaxed and well rested, the trials and tribulations of life
are much easier to face, and it is with this in mind that I have sought out
a multitude of beautiful and inspirational ideas guaranteed to transform
our places of sleep into havens of rest. A shaped upholstered headboard
in a favorite fabric can change a bed from the ordinary to the unique,
while a flowing, elegant bed canopy will convert an ordinary studio bed
into a luxurious retreat. This book contains twenty inspirational and
achievable projects, each accompanied with clear and easy-to-follow
step-by-step instructions. I hope it will encourage you to turn your own
bedroom into a more comfortable, inviting, and stylish space.

Katrin Cargill

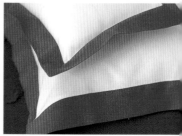

above left Checks and stripes in combination are unified by the use of a blue and white color scheme throughout.
left Delicate white thread embroidery enlivens the edges of a crisp cotton sheet and matching pillowcase.
below left Using ties as a fastening is a simple solution to closing covers and cases as well as an attractive decorative addition. Either make them in a contrasting fabric or use the same material for a more subtle form of embellishment.

top right The simple geometric designs of the decorative stitching on these pillowcases perfectly complements the colors and shapes of the patchwork bedspread.
above right A hot pink flanged border adds a bold and colorful note to an otherwise plain pair of white pillowcases.
below right The regimented stripes and precisely squared ends of this plump bolster are the perfect match for the sheet beneath, giving the bed an air of tailored elegance.

above Quilted fabric with an unusual textural quality adds interest to a pillow and creates a comfortable feel.
left Linen pillowcases and sheets are the ultimate luxury. This linen pillowcase is held closed by floppy linen bows; a soft, informal look perfect for a bedroom.

pillows and sheets A bedroom is

a place for sleep, but it is also a room where you can be a little self-indulgent with your forms of decoration. Don't just stick to the usual plain bed dressings. Instead use checks or stripes to add a simple yet eye-catching area of interest. If this seems too adventurous, introduce more subtle decorative touches, such as an embroidered or contrasting border around the edges of sheets, or ties and buttons on pillows.

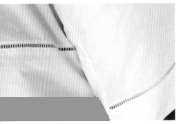

above left Lacy delicate cutwork on starched white cotton is a bed linen classic. Here a pretty daisy pattern adorns the border of a large square pillowcase.
above right An impromtu bolster case is constructed from a piece of white cotton loosely tied with a peach satin ribbon.
left A dainty drawn threadwork border embellishes these matching pillowcases. The crisp cool cotton of the bed linen is teamed with a vivid red bedspread for a cozy countrified effect.

striped silk bolster

This chic and stylish yet invitingly plump bolster cover is
made from colorful striped raw silk. The mouthwatering sherbet
shades of the stripes and the excess material bunched at each end
of the bolster make it reminiscent of an enormous bonbon. Covering
the buttons in exactly the same fabric and matching the color
of each button to a stripe is well worth the effort, as such details
add to the overall effect of glossy elegance.

materials & equipment

bolster pad

silk striped fabric

approximately 18 buttons

instructions under flap ➤

1 Measure the length and circumference of the bolster pad to estimate fabric quantities. The fabric must be 45 inches longer than the bolster and 12 inches wider than the circumference measurement. Press under a double 2-inch hem along one long edge of the fabric. Machine stitch in place. Along the other long edge, press a 2-inch double hem. Slipstitch this hem in place.

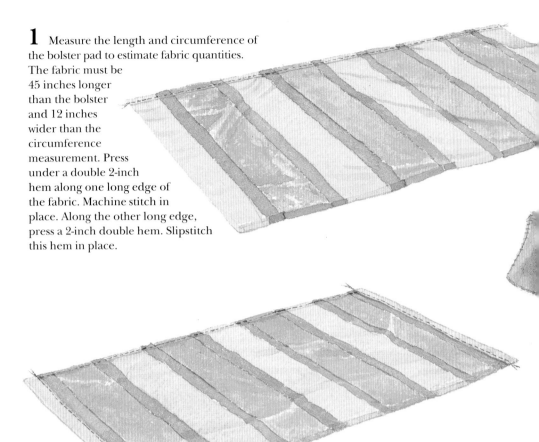

2 At both short ends of the fabric, turn under and press a double 1-inch hem. Machine stitch the hem in place, close to the inner folded edge.

3 Lay the fabric flat, right side up. Along the machine-stitched edge, mark points for the buttons, approximately 4 inches in from the edge and 4 inches apart. Cover the buttons in the silk fabric, matching the color of each button to the color of a stripe. Sew each button over its matching stripe.

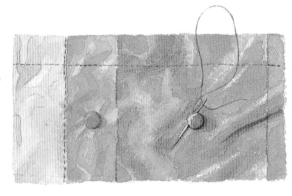

4 Turn the fabric over and place it wrong side up. Position the bolster in the center of the fabric and wrap the fabric around it. Mark the position of each buttonhole on the fabric directly above the corresponding button. Remove the bolster and sew over the mark with small basting stitches. Make sure that the marked buttonholes are the correct size for the diameter of the buttons.

ticking with binding

These practical and hardwearing cotton ticking pillowcases have
been enlivened by the addition of jazzy red binding tape. A classic
rectangular pillowcase is decorated with broad parallel stripes, while
a square case has a flanged, trimmed border. Imaginative use of
trimmings will make an ordinary pillowcase unique, so why not really
go to town and experiment with bold patterned braid, broad velvet
ribbon, shaggy fringe or even a ball fringe.

materials & equipment

cotton ticking fabric

binding tape in a contrasting color

instructions under flap ➤

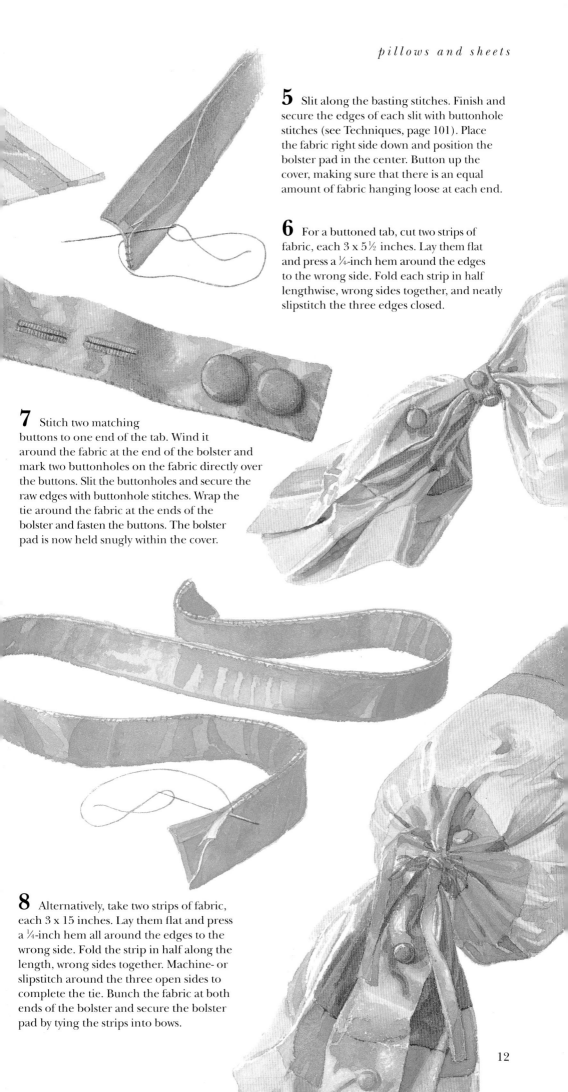

5 Slit along the basting stitches. Finish and secure the edges of each slit with buttonhole stitches (see Techniques, page 101). Place the fabric right side down and position the bolster pad in the center. Button up the cover, making sure that there is an equal amount of fabric hanging loose at each end.

6 For a buttoned tab, cut two strips of fabric, each 3 x 5½ inches. Lay them flat and press a ¼-inch hem around the edges to the wrong side. Fold each strip in half lengthwise, wrong sides together, and neatly slipstitch the three edges closed.

7 Stitch two matching buttons to one end of the tab. Wind it around the fabric at the end of the bolster and mark two buttonholes on the fabric directly over the buttons. Slit the buttonholes and secure the raw edges with buttonhole stitches. Wrap the tie around the fabric at the ends of the bolster and fasten the buttons. The bolster pad is now held snugly within the cover.

8 Alternatively, take two strips of fabric, each 3 x 15 inches. Lay them flat and press a ¼-inch hem all around the edges to the wrong side. Fold the strip in half along the length, wrong sides together. Machine- or slipstitch around the three open sides to complete the tie. Bunch the fabric at both ends of the bolster and secure the bolster pad by tying the strips into bows.

piqué pillows with bows

These inviting brown gingham pillowcases are extremely easy to make, especially if you use extra-wide sheeting, as you only need a single piece of fabric that is twice the width of the pillow. The piqué panels, held in place with matching gingham bows, lend the pillowcases a demure air of modesty and old-fashioned charm.

materials & equipment

cotton gingham fabric

cotton piqué fabric

instructions under flap ➤

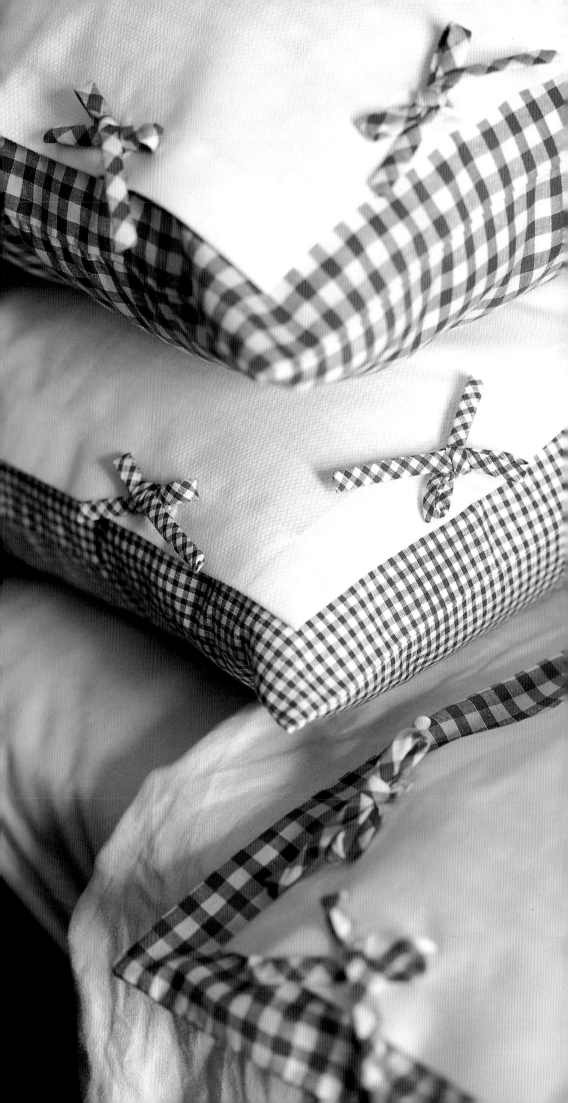

velvet-edged pillowcase

A casual striped-cotton pillowcase with unexpected decorative elements – a vibrant velvet ribbon trim that emphasizes a flanged border cut from the same fabric, but with a contrasting horizontal stripe. Paired with similarly trimmed white bed linen, this stylish pillowcase will add a touch of style to the simplest bedroom.

materials & equipment

striped Indian cotton

¾-inch wide velvet ribbon

instructions under flap ➤

red-trimmed linen

Cool linen sheets and pillowcases are irresistibly inviting after a long day. Here, square pillows have been encased in linen pillowcases trimmed with boldly colored faggotting for a cozy, countrified effect. Teamed with a matching sheet and a simple gingham bedspread, they bring a charming air of simplicity to a bedroom.

materials & equipment

white cotton or linen fabric

¾-inch wide trim

instructions under flap ➤

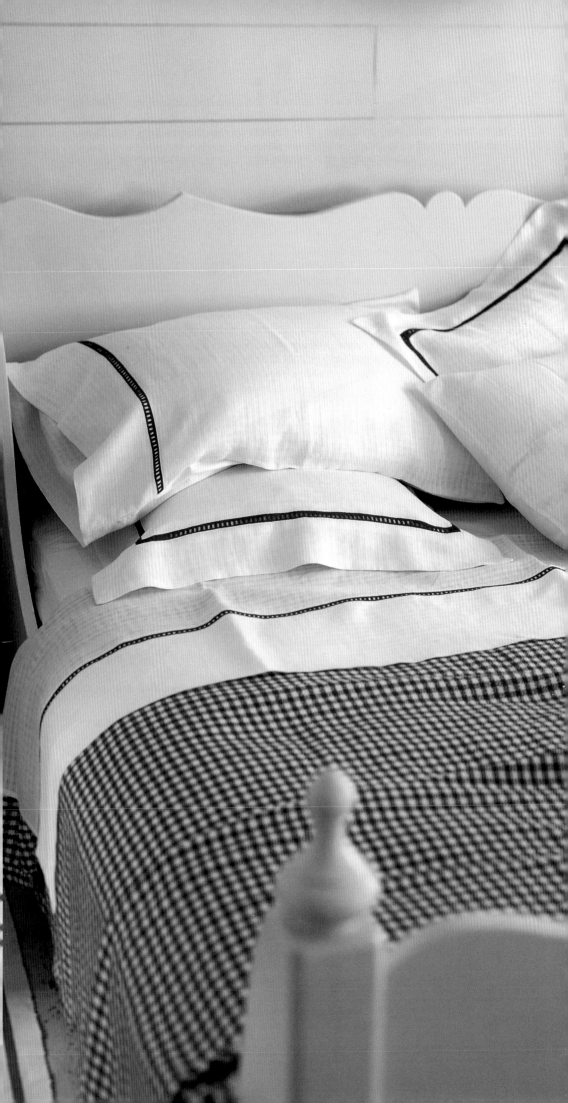

right A plump feather eiderdown covered in gingham makes a snug and warm winter bedspread. The channel quilting holds the filling in place and prevents it from lumping.

below Crocheted cotton bedspreads are available in a wide choice of patterns and colors. This is a fine example of intricate white-on-white crochet work, topped with a cotton bolster.

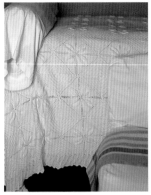

bedspreads

Bedspreads have a dual function: to provide warmth and decoration. Whether your preference is for dainty florals or tailored stripes, your bedspread must be both attractive and inviting, and its fabric and design should suggest comfort and luxuriousness.

above left Graphic stripes and unusual surface texturing enhance a simple sleigh bed.

above center A complementary colored checked border and a matching appliquéd crown motif give an old wool blanket a new lease on life.

above right A boldly checked black and ecru comforter creates a cozy yet contemporary effect.

left A floral cotton sheet with ruffled border makes a pretty summer bedspread.

top left Quilted blue and white checks are smartly teamed with ticking.
top center A crisp white cotton bedspread made from Marseilles cloth. Jacquard would create a similar effect.
top right A faded country quilt to snuggle up beneath.
left This colorful bedspread is cleverly constructed from remnants of antique ticking.
below A fine wool blanket embellished with decorative embroidery and a loopy trim.
bottom left Delicate lace work has an air of distinction.
bottom right An antique floral comforter with a beguiling air of old-fashioned charm.

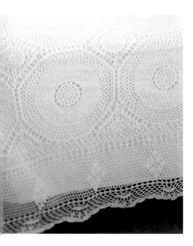

appliquéd matelasse bedspread

This bedspread is made from matelasse, a thick double cloth with a quilted effect. A crisp blue-striped ribbon has been appliquéd to the bedspread in a bold and geometric pattern of squares. It is essential that the bedspread itself is an exact square, so no unevenly sized squares or crooked lines can mar its perfection.

materials & equipment

85 x 85 inches matelasse fabric

27 yards striped ribbon

instructions under flap ➤

feather-stitched patchwork quilt

This cozy patchwork quilt, made from scraps and remnants
of antique blue and white printed cotton, is not handstitched in the
traditional way. Instead, the quilt is machine sewn to save time and
effort. Feather stitching in a complementary color meanders over
and around the seams, providing a decorative finishing touch.

materials & equipment

a wide variety of scraps and remnants of fabric for the patchwork

batting

backing fabric for the quilt

embroidery needle

embroidery thread

instructions under flap ➤

oak-leaf stenciled duvet

The simple but effective craft of stenciling is not limited to walls and woodwork. A little imagination and a stencil kit are all that are needed to transform a plain duvet into something totally unique. Here, garlands of oak leaves have been stenciled on to a cotton-ticking duvet in washable fabric paint.

materials & equipment

cotton ticking fabric

stencil-making kit

washable white, gray, and black paint

stencil brush

thin brush

plain fabric for border and ties

instructions under flap ➤

velvet-edged bedspread

This lightweight summer bedspread is made from a crisp striped cotton and edged with a narrow brown velvet piping for an effect that is both simple and sophisticated. The bedspread is only intended to fall halfway to the floor on each side, drawing attention to the rhythmic curves of the neatly piped scalloped edging.

materials & equipment

striped cotton fabric

velvet piping

instructions under flap ➤

dust ruffles serve a practical purpose, concealing

unattractive bed bases, stumpy bed legs, and underbed storage areas. In recent years, over-elaborate versions in flouncy, fussy designs have earned dust ruffles a bad reputation. However, this is undeserved, for a tailored dust ruffle with inverted pleats can be extremely elegant, while a delicate antique lace-trimmed dust ruffle will add distinction to any bedroom.

left and above Fine organza with a deep double hem billows out beneath a simple wooden-framed bed. Despite its fragile, flimsy appearance, organza is extremely strong, making it a luxurious yet practical choice for home furnishings. *below* In a guest bedroom, a blue and white theme boldly combines checks, stripes, and flowers, and demonstrates how different patterns can be harmoniously linked by color alone. This stylish effect has been achieved on a tight budget – the dust ruffles are fashioned from humble dishtowels.

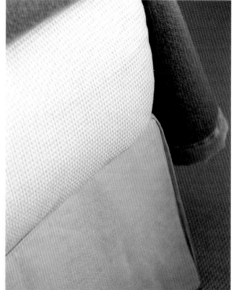

above The graphic lines of this bold red-and-white checked dust ruffle are softened by the unexpected addition of a soft white lace trim at the top.
below left and right A colorful red-and-white checked cotton is folded into precise box pleats in this cheerful version, which makes the bed the focal point in this small bedroom.

bottom left A delicate white scalloped sheet used as a dust ruffle hangs just above floor level, peeping out from under an exquisitely detailed bedspread.
above right A simple yet sophisticated linen dust ruffle with an inverted pleat at the corners adds a unfussy note of comfort to a cool, contemporary interior.

tailored pictorial print

Toile de Jouy, a cotton fabric printed with idyllic pastoral scenes in muted tones, is ideally suited to a relaxed and soothing bedroom environment. If it is made into frilly bed dressings, the effect can be a little too fussy. However, *toile de Jouy* is perfect for the simple uncluttered lines of this precisely pleated dust ruffle.

materials & equipment

toile de Jouy *fabric*

lining fabric

piping cord

bias binding

instructions under flap ➤

soft green scallops

This simple but decorative scalloped dust ruffle is designed
especially for a day bed with a headboard and footboard, and
is the perfect partner for the scalloped corona (see pages 82–84).
However, the dust ruffle looks equally effective on its own, and is
guaranteed to add an air of elegant simplicity to any bedroom.
If you have an ordinary bed without a footboard, add a third
section of scalloped skirt for the end of the bed.

materials & equipment

cotton fabric

lining fabric

instructions under flap ➤

appliquéd zigzags

This bold dust ruffle, with its zigzagged edges, strikes a note of warmth and vitality in an otherwise cool and uncluttered bedroom. The hot pink color and solid shapes of the dust ruffle are a perfect foil for the graceful fluid outline of an antique brass bedstead. A checked fabric, which harmonizes perfectly with the pink of the dust ruffle, has been used for the duvet and cut into diamond-shaped patches that are used to appliqué the bottom edge.

materials & equipment

solid-color cotton fabric

checked or gingham cotton

lining fabric

instructions under flap ➤

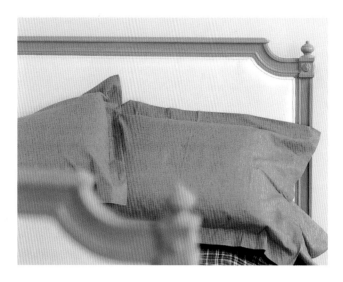

headboards
Without a headboard, a bed can have a rather forlorn, unfinished appearance, while an attractive headboard makes any bed a focal point. Upholstered headboards lend themselves to all kinds of imaginative treatments and can be matched to other furnishings for an integrated effect.

left Natural textures and geometric shapes combine to create a coolly contemporary look in this stylish bedroom. The oversized headboard, upholstered in beige cotton and covered with a white cotton panel, provides an unobtrusive backdrop for the luxurious bed. *above left* Wooden headboards with an upholstered panel in the center are extremely versatile – a change of fabric on the panels will completely transform the character of the bed. Here, a plain white cotton panel draws attention to the elegant lines of the carved wooden bedframe. *above right* A plumply padded headboard is upholstered in an abstract print. Matching piping on the back and front of the headboard emphasizes the shaped corners. *below right* On a kingsize bed, the sheer size of the headboard can be overpowering, but here the effect is minimized by the use of a pretty *toile de Jouy* fabric and by shaping the sides to make the headboard appear narrower.

above A narrow red stripe creates an elegant tailored effect on a rectangular headboard. The narrow piping provides a chic yet subtle finishing touch. Crisp white cotton bed linen is the perfect partner for this stylish headboard.

florals and checks

This padded and shaped headboard is covered with a slipcover made from an 1950s-style printed fabric that combines small checks with rose-scattered stripes. Although the headboard will add a note of coziness and comfort to any bedroom, it is ideally suited to a guest room, for the warm colors and the pretty fabric make it particularly inviting. For a simpler, more formal effect, choose a solid color and team it with boldly colored contrasting piping and ties.

materials & equipment

¼-inch thick plywood for the headboard

medium-grade sandpaper

4-ounce batting

wood glue

staple gun

printed cotton fabric

lining fabric

contrasting piping

instructions under flap ➤

tie-on padding

Tie-on padding is an inexpensive and stylish way of creating
a cozy, comfortable headboard. The concept is extremely simple –
a square of padding is covered in striped cotton and tied to a simple
headboard, creating an inviting and luxurious effect. The beauty
of this idea lies in its versatility – the mood of a bedroom can be
completely transformed in a moment by changing the padded
panel for one covered with a different pattern or color.

materials & equipment

for the headboard:

¾-inch thick plywood for the headboard

4-ounce batting

wood glue

lining fabric

staple gun

wood for struts

for the tie-on padding:

4-ounce batting

striped cotton fabric for the slipcover and ties

instructions under flap ➤

hanging headboards

Suspended from wooden pegs, these two hanging panels
provide an attractive alternative to a traditional headboard. The long
panels have a tailored appearance and draw attention to the plump
pillows and invitingly crisp white sheets on the bed below. They
would look just as striking and effective above twin beds.

materials & equipment

thick cotton fabric

cotton fabric for the inset border and lining

striped cotton fabric for the outer border

instructions under flap ➤

daisy motif headboard

The elegant and unusual outline of this upholstered headboard will add a touch of grandeur to even the smallest bedroom. The headboard has been plumply padded for comfort and then tightly covered with a small-checked cotton fabric. Finally, a daisy motif has been picked out in shiny upholstery tacks.

materials & equipment

¾-inch thick plywood for the headboard

medium-grade sandpaper

4-ounce batting

wood glue

staple gun

heavy cotton fabric

upholstery tacks in a color to match the main fabric

instructions under flap ➤

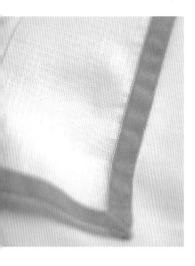

canopies add drama and

romance to a bedroom. Even an ordinary studio bed can be transformed by the addition of flowing drapes. A corona creates a formal, elegant effect, while a simple mosquito net suspended above the bed adds a hint of colonial style. What could be more soothing than drifting off to sleep cocooned in layers of gently flowing fabric?

left and above A fine organza canopy softens the minimalist squiggles of a metal bed. The fabric has been sewn to a hoop suspended from the ceiling. The edges and bottom of the canopy are edged in narrow gold velvet ribbon, adding a touch of luxury to a cool white scheme. The crisp white cotton bed linen is edged in matching gold ribbon, unifying the scheme. *right* A magnificent Shaker cherrywood four-poster is adorned with a panel of bold checks and subtle stripes, loosely knotted to a horizontal support. The practical ties mean that the panel can be easily removed for seasonal changes or laundering.

left and above A modern metal four-poster with clean minimalist lines is softened with delicate drapery made of hemmed organza and an intricate lace bedspread, which create an ethereal feel without concealing the elegant lines of the bed.

scalloped corona

A corona brings a regal and elegant air to any bed, and has the
ability to transform the most ordinary of bedrooms into a luxurious
retreat. The elegant carved-wood corona shown in the picture below
is a traditional Swedish design. Similar ready-made coronas can be
difficult to find, so here I show how to create the effect using a corona
board made from plywood and concealed by a scalloped valance,
which adds a majestic finishing touch.

materials & equipment

¾-inch thick plywood for the corona board

angled brackets

flexible curtain track

curtain hooks

woven checked cotton fabric

1-inch wide gathering tape

¾-inch wide velcro fastening

instructions under flap ➤

flowered voile
bed canopy

This simple arrangement in floaty floral voile brings romance and
elegance to a bedroom without looking too fussy and flouncy.
The abundant quantities of voile cascade gently from a short length
of curtain pole that has been attached to the wall with a bracket and
finished with an unobtrusive finial to keep the gathered voile in place.

materials & equipment

floral voile

plain cotton for lining

short wooden curtain pole with bracket and finial

instructions under flap ➤

tied-on bed hangings

Four-posters are often associated with grand, formal bed dressings, but here the austere lines of a very contemporary metal-framed four-poster are softened by eight cotton panels loosely tied to the top of the bed frame. As both sides of the hangings are visible, a woven check fabric has been used to dispense with the need for lining.

materials & equipment

thick checked madras cotton

bias binding in a contrasting color

instructions under flap ➤

striped scalloped canopy

This scalloped bed canopy, with its bold blocks of color, has a cheerful and pleasing simplicity that complements the robust lines of a Shaker-style wooden four-poster bed perfectly. The scalloped canopy is lined and hangs down over the horizontal supports of the bed frame, lending enough weight to hold the canopy in place.

materials & equipment

white linen

colored linen

lining fabric

instructions under flap ➤

equipment and techniques

Basic equipment

To make the projects in this book, you will need some basic tools. A pair of good-quality cutting shears are essential, as are some medium-sized dressmaker's scissors and small embroidery scissors. Equally important are a metal tape measure, steel yardstick and a small plastic ruler, which will allow you to measure accurately and to double-check all measurements. Invest in some good-quality steel dressmaker's pins, which will not rust, and keep them in a box so they stay sharp. A steam iron will prove invaluable during the assembly process, but should be used with a damp cloth to protect delicate fabrics. For marking fabrics, vanishing fabric pens are easy to apply, and the ink fades away after 72 hours. A metal thimble is another useful item, as is a knitting needle to coax ties right side out.

Some of the projects in this book involve making a headboard from plywood. To cut the plywood to the required shape, you will need a small saw, and fabric glue is necessary to attach padding or lining to the board. Securing fabric to a headboard may require the use of a heavy-duty staple gun. You will also need a hammer, a drill, and an assortment of nails and screws for hanging drapes and coronas or attaching headboards to beds.

The projects in this book involve both hand and machine sewing, and a sewing machine is needed to make most items. Although it is possible to make many of the items featured by hand, it would be a long and laborious process. Your sewing machine should have a good selection of basic stitches. Sophisticated accessories are not necessary, but a piping foot is required for some of the projects in the book.

Finally, the process of making bed linen will be much easier and more enjoyable if you are able to work in a well-lit, well-ventilated area and have access to a large work table.

Choosing fabric

For each project the fabrics are specified, as the weight, texture, and pattern is suited to the particular design. If you want to choose an alternative material, always try to select fabric of a similar weight. You should always check that your chosen fabric is preshrunk and fade-resistant.

Before you cut into the fabric, lay it out on a flat surface and check it carefully for any flaws. Some minor flaws can sometimes be hidden in hems or seams. If the fabric is badly flawed, you should return it to the manufacturer or retailer.

You may find cleaning instructions printed on the selvages of many fabrics. Any lined items should always be dry cleaned, as lining fabric and main fabric tend to shrink at different rates when washed.

The fire-retardant qualities of upholstery fabrics are governed by legislation in most countries. We suggest that you obtain advice from a retailer to make sure that your chosen fabric is in line with these regulations.

Measuring for bed linen

Before you embark on any of the projects in this book, you must first accurately measure the bed that you intend to furnish. This is essential since it will allow you to calculate the size of the finished item and work out how much fabric you will need to make it. Always take measurements with a steel tape measure (plastic ones can stretch and become inaccurate) and get someone to help you if the bed is a large one.

Measuring for a pillowcase
Measure the width and length of the pillow. Add a 10 inch flap and seam allowance to the width and 1½ inches to the length, unless otherwise stated in a project.

Measuring for a duvet
Measure the comforter across the width and length. Add 2 inches to each measurement.

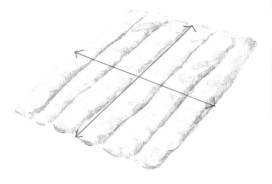

Measuring for a bedspread
Measure the bed with bedclothes and pillows in place. For the length, measure from the bedhead to the floor at the foot of the bed. Add an extra 12 inches to tuck behind the pillows. For the width, measure from the floor on one side of the bed over the bed to the floor on the other side. Seam allowances are given in the individual projects.

Measuring for a dust ruffle
Measure the bed base without the mattress. For the length of the central panel (which lies beneath the mattress) measure the head to the foot of the bed. For the width, measure from one side of the bed base to the other. For the depth of the skirt, measure from the top of the bed base to the floor. The amount of fabric required for the skirt will depend on the fullness of the dust ruffle. Seam allowances are given in the individual projects.

Measuring for a headboard
In order to calculate the width of the headboard, you must first measure the width of the bed. The headboard must be the same width as the bed from side edge to side edge. It should be approximately 3 feet tall, but the height and shape of the headboard can be adjusted, depending on the effect you wish to achieve. Take into account the size of your bed – a tiny bed will need a lower headboard and vice versa.

Making a headboard
Cut a piece of plywood to the required proportions and smooth any rough edges with sandpaper. For a shaped headboard, make a template and scale it up to the desired size (see Templates, page 104). Cut a piece of paper or cardboard to the size of the headboard and draw, trace, or photocopy the desired shape onto the paper. Cut out the template and attach it to the headboard. Draw all around it with a pencil or marker pen, then cut all along the marked line, using a small saw. Sand the edges.
Cover the headboard in lining or in main fabric and attach it to the bed with two strips of wood, each about 3 inches wide and 1 inch thick. Saw a long notch in one end of each strip so it will slot over the screws on the back of the bed base. Measure the distance between these screws so you will know how far apart to set the wooden strips.

Measuring for bed hangings

If you have a four-poster bed, measure the drop from the bottom of the horizontal supports to the floor for the length of the bedhangings, and the distance between the vertical supports for the width.

If you wish to make a corona or other wall-mounted bed draperies, it is much easier to measure and calculate fabric quantities once the pole or corona board is mounted in place. As a rough guide, they should be positioned approximately 12 inches below the ceiling, but this measurement may have to be adjusted, depending on the proportions of the room. Mount any fixtures to the wall securely, using sturdy brackets that will be able to bear the weight of the fixture plus several yards of fabric.

Cutting out the fabric

When making bed linen, or any home furnishing, it is essential that fabric is cut straight, or the finished item will hang crookedly. Unroll or unfold the fabric on a flat surface. Use a carpenter's square and metal ruler to mark a straight line in pencil or fabric pen across the width on the wrong side of the fabric.

To cut a width of fabric in half, fold it selvage to selvage, then press. Carefully cut along the pressed fold line. If you are using fabric with a high sheen or pile, mark the top of each

width with a notch so you can make sure all the fabric will run in the right direction on the finished item.

Joining widths

When making duvets, sheets, and bedspreads, always place a full-width panel in the center of the item with equal part or whole widths joined on each side. To join widths, place one width on top of another, right sides facing, and pin, baste, and machine stitch the widths together, using a straight ⅜-inch seam. Trim away any surplus fabric and clip the seams to prevent any puckering or bunching.

Matching patterns

To match patterns across several widths of fabric, fold under a ⅜-inch seam allowance on one width of fabric and press. Place the other width on a flat surface, right side up. Take the width with the folded edge and place it on top of the second width of fabric. Match the pattern. Fold the top piece of fabric so the two pieces are right sides together, then seam down the fold line. Open the seam and press it flat.

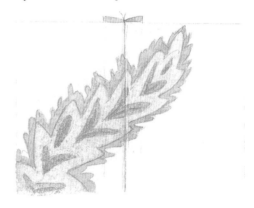

BASIC SEWING TECHNIQUES

Stitches

Basting stitch

This temporary stitch holds fabric in place until it is permanently secured. Knot the end of the thread and take large loose stitches. Use a bright-colored thread so the basting is easy to spot and can be removed quickly after the permanent stitching has been done.

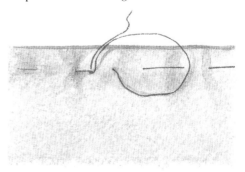

Slipstitch

Slipstitch holds a folded edge to flat fabric or two folded edges together, as in a mitered corner. Work on the wrong side of the fabric from right to left. Start with the needle in the fold. Push it out and pick up a few threads from the flat fabric, then insert it into the hem again, all in one continuous movement. The stitches should be almost invisible.

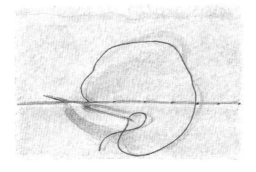

Herringbone stitch

This stitch is used to hold a raw edge to flat fabric. Work from left to right on the wrong side of the fabric. Start with the needle in the fold of the hem. Push it through the fold fabric and bring the needle diagonally up to the flat fabric. Take a small backward stitch in the flat fabric, approximately ¼ inch above the fold, picking up a couple of threads. Bring the needle diagonally back down to the fold and make a small backward stitch of equal size to the previous one through one thickness of the fabric.

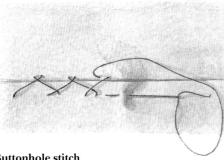

Buttonhole stitch

This stitch is both decorative and strengthening since it prevents the buttonhole from fraying. It can also be used wherever a raw edge needs to be finished or secured. Work on the right side of the fabric, using a short needle and a strong thread with

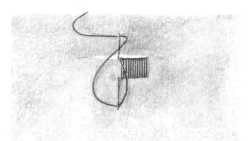

a knotted end. Stitch with the raw edge uppermost. Push the needle through the fabric, from back to front, approximately ⅛ inch below the raw edge of the buttonhole. Twist the thread around the tip of the needle, then pull the needle through to form a knot at the raw edge of the fabric. Always keep the stitches evenly spaced. Some sewing machines have a very useful buttonhole attachment.

Feather stitch

This decorative stitch should be worked in silk embroidery thread on the right side of the fabric. It is easiest to do if you are following a straight line, such as a seam, and can imagine that there is a parallel line about ¼ inch above and below the seam. Bring the needle through the fabric at A and insert it into the fabric at B. Bring it out again at C, looping the thread under the needle before pulling it through. Repeat the process by inserting the needle again at D, emerging again at E, then looping the thread beneath the needle again. Continue to repeat this pattern, always alternating the looped stitches to alternate sides of the central line.

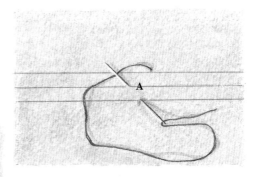

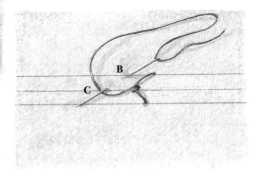

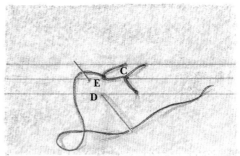

Seams

Flat seam

This seam is used to join pieces of fabric. Place the two pieces of fabric right sides together, aligning the edges that are to be seamed. Pin and baste, then machine stitch the seam. Reverse the stitches at the beginning and end of the seam to secure it in place. Press the seam flat against the wrong side of the material for a neat finish.

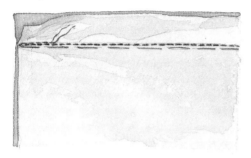

Flat fell seam

This is a sturdy seam for joining heavy fabric. Join two pieces of fabric with a flat seam. Press the seam to one side. Trim the underneath seam to half its width. Fold the upper seam allowance over the trimmed one and baste. Machine stitch a second seam all the way along the folded edge.

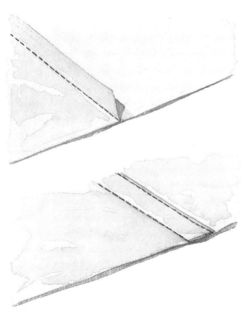

French seam

This self-finishing seam contains all raw edges and is used to join sheers and other lightweight fabrics. Place two pieces of fabric wrong sides together, aligning the raw edges that are to be seamed. Pin, baste, and machine stitch a narrow seam close to the raw edge. Trim the seam allowance. Fold the material right sides together and pin,

baste, and machine stitch a second seam ⅜ inch from the first, enclosing all raw edges in a narrow tube of fabric.

Double hem

A double hem encloses raw edges and lies flat against the back of fabric. For a 4-inch double hem, the hem allowance will be 8 inches. Press the hem allowance along the edge of the fabric. Open out the hem and fold the raw edge up to the pressed line. Fold again and secure in place.

Mitering corners

Mitering is the neatest way of working hem corners. Press in the hem allowance along the bottom and sides of the fabric, then open it out flat again. Where the two fold lines meet, turn in the corner of the fabric diagonally. Turn in the hems along the pressed fold to form a neat diagonal line. Use slipstitch to secure the miter.

Making an angled miter

An angled miter is necessary when a double bottom hem is wider than the side hems. Press the hem allowances, then open out again. Fold in the corner toward the bottom hem. Then make the first fold in the double hem. Fold in the side hem, then make the second fold in the double hem. The folded edges should meet.

Making bias binding

Bias binding is an effective and attractive way to enclose raw edges of fabric. It is available ready made in a wide choice of colors, but it is quick and easy to make your own. Place your chosen fabric on a flat surface, with the wrong side up. Fold one corner of the fabric diagonally until the end is aligned with the selvage, forming a triangle of fabric. The diagonal fold line is the bias line of the fabric. Mark strips parallel to the bias line all the way across the fabric and cut them out.

To make one continous strip of bias binding, join the strips. Take two strips and place them right sides together at right angles, lining up the raw edges. Pin and machine stitch across the width, using a ⅜-inch seam allowance. Trim the seams, press flat, and trim the corners.

Making ties and tabs

To make a tie, cut a strip of material to the desired width and length. Fold the strip in half along the length, wrong sides together, and press. Pin, baste, and machine sew all along the long side and one short end. Leave one end unstitched. Push the tie right side out with the aid of a knitting needle. Turn a ¼-inch fold to the inside of the tie, press in place, and slipstitch the end closed. Tabs can be made in exactly the same way as ties – the only difference is that the strip of fabric is wider so they are generally buttoned, not tied.

Making piping

Piping is made from a length of piping cord covered with bias binding. The binding must be wide enough to cover the cord and to allow a ⅜-inch seam allowance on each side of it. Place the cord in the middle of the wrong side of the binding and wrap the binding so the cord is enclosed. Baste close to the cord. Machine stitch close to the cord using a piping foot.

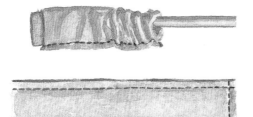

templates

All the templates in this book must be enlarged. Either use a photocopier to enlarge the template to the desired proportions (sometimes stated in the individual project) on heavy paper or cardboard, or trace the pattern on graph paper, increase the proportions to the desired size, then transfer to heavy paper or cardboard. Cut out the template. Pin it to the wrong side of the fabric, then mark all the way around the outline of the template in vanishing fabric pen.

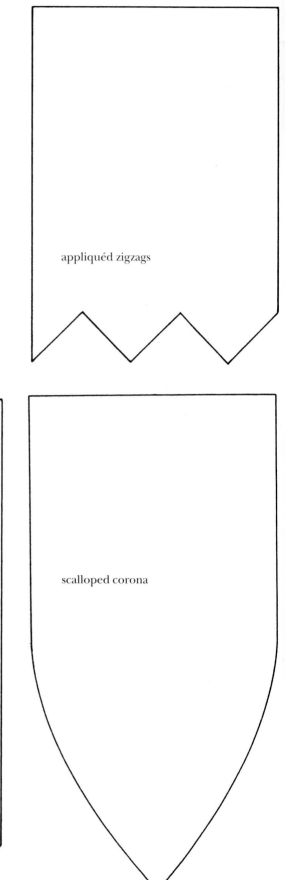

appliquéd zigzags

striped scalloped canopy

scalloped corona

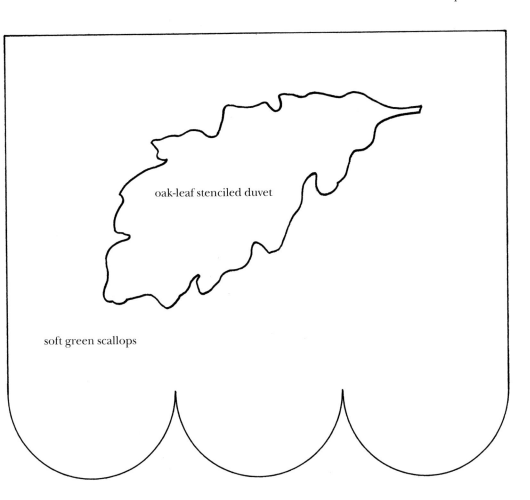

oak-leaf stenciled duvet

soft green scallops

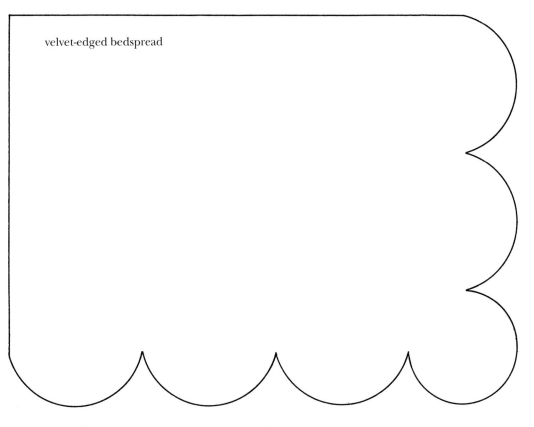

velvet-edged bedspread

directory of suppliers

* an asterisk denotes trade only. Contact the address given for your nearest supplier.

fabrics

Laura Ashley
414 Madison Avenue
New York
NY 10021

B & J Fabric
263 West 40th Street
New York
NY 10018

Boussac of France*
979 Third Avenue
New York
NY 10022

Brunschwig & Fils*
979 Third Avenue
New York
NY 10022

Calico Corners
203 Gale Lane
Kennett Square
PA 19348

Jane Churchill-Wish*
distributed by
Cowtan & Tout, Inc*
979 Third Avenue
New York NY 10022

**Clarence House
Fabrics, Ltd***
211 East 58th Street
New York
NY 10022

Colefax & Fowler*
distributed by
Cowtan & Tout, Inc*
979 Third Avenue
New York
NY 10022

Covington Fabrics*
15 East 26th Street
New York
NY 10010

Cowtan & Tout, Inc*
979 Third Avenue
New York
NY 10022

Designers Guild*
distributed by
Osborne & Little*
979 Third Avenue
New York
NY 10022

Pierre Deux
870 Madison Avenue
New York
NY 10021

The Fabric Center
485 Electric Avenue

Fitchburg
MA 01420

Pierre Frey*
distributed by Fonthill
979 Third Avenue
New York
NY 10022

Hinson & Co*
979 Third Avenue
New York
NY 10022

Keepsake Quilting
Route 25B
P.O. Box 1618
Center Harbour
NH 03226-1618

**Ralph Lauren
Home Collection**
*979 Third Avenue
New York
NY 10022
980 Madison Avenue
New York
NY 10021
867 Madison Avenue
New York
NY 10021

**Ian Mankin at
Coconut Co.**
129-131 Greene Street
New York
NY 10012-8080

Oppenheim's
P. O. Box 29
120 East Main Street
North Manchester
IN 46962-0052

Osborne & Little*
979 Third Avenue
New York
NY 10022

Randolph & Hein
1 Arkansas Street
San Francisco
CA 94107

Scalamandre Silk, Inc.*
950 Third Avenue
New York
NY 10022

Sanderson*
979 Third Avenue
New York
NY 10022

F. Schumacher & Co.*
79 Madison Avenue
New York
N Y 10016

Smith & Noble
P. O. Box 1387
Corona
CA 91718

Thai Silks!
252 State Street
Los Altos
CA 94022

Waverley Fabrics*
79 Madison Avenue
New York
NY 10016

notions and trims

Clothilde, Inc.
2 Sew Smart Way
Stevens Point
WI 54481-8031

Conso Products
P.O. Box 326
Union
SC 29379

Hollywood Trims
Prym-Dritz Corporation
P.O. Box 5028
Spartanburg
SC 29304

Houlés, Inc.*
8584 Melrose Avenue
Los Angeles
CA 90069

Nancy's Notions
P.O. Box 683
Beaver Dam
WI 53916

C.M. Offray & Sons, Inc.
Route 24
P.O. Box 601
Chester
NJ 07930

Tinsel Trading Co.
47 West 38th Street
New York
NY 10018

pillows

A.B.C. Carpet & Home
88 Broadway
New York
NY 10011

Bloomingdales
1000 Third Avenue
New York
NY 10022

Gracious Homes
1220 Third Avenue
New York
NY 10021

Charlotte Moss
1027 Lexington Avenue
New York
NY 10011

Nicholas*
979 Third Avenue
New York
NY 10022

The Pillowry
1132 East 61st Street
New York
NY 10021

Pillow Finery*
979 Third Avenue
New York
NY 10022

John Rosselli
523 East 73rd Street
New York
NY 10021

credits

Front cover picture: fabric from Cath Kidston, headboard made by Cover Up Designs of Kingsclere, pillowcase and pink blanket from Designers Guild

page 1 antique quilt from Nicole Fabre, ticking from Malabar Cotton Company
page 2 bedhangings from John Lewis, bed and sheets from Shaker
page 4 from left to right: fabrics from Osborne & Little; fabric from Sanderson, stripes from F. R. Street; plain fabric from Malabar Cotton Company, checked fabric from Designers Guild
page 5 from left to right: plain fabrics from Osborne & Little, striped fabric from Malabar Cotton Company; checked fabric from Ian Mankin, dust ruffle fabric from Osborne & Little; fabric from Designers Guild, trimming from V. V. Rouleaux, blanket from Ralph Lauren Home
page 6 sheet from Ralph Lauren Home
page 7 voile fabric from Osborne & Little, lining fabric from Designers Guild

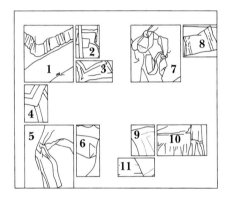

pillows and sheets pages 8–9
1 antique textiles from Tobias & the Angel
2 sheets from Shaker
3 pillowcases from Designers Guild
4 bed linen from Harrods
5 fabric from Designers Guild
6 antique bolster from Pimpernel & Partners
7 pillowcase by Damask
8 pillow from Pierre Frey
9, 10, 11 assortment of antique linens from Lunn Antiques

projects: *striped silk bolster:* fabric from Designers Guild • *ticking with binding:* fabric from Malabar Cotton Company, trimming from John Lewis • *piqué pillows with bows:* both fabrics from McCulloch & Wallis • *velvet-edged pillowcase:* fabric from Ian Mankin, velvet trimming from V. V. Rouleaux, antique linen sheet from Tobias & the Angel • *red-trimmed linen:* fabric from Designers Guild, trimming from V. V. Rouleaux

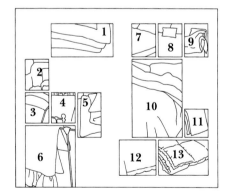

bedspreads pages 30–31
1 fabric from Shaker
2 crocheted bedspread from Liberty
3 quilt from The Conran Shop
4 blanket from Tobias & the Angel, fabric from McKinney & Co
5 fabric from Ian Mankin
6 sheet from Ralph Lauren Home
7 antique quilt from Nicole Fabre, ticking from Malabar Cotton Company
8 bedspread from Lunn Antiques
9 quilt from Damask
10 antique bedspread from Pimpernel & Partners
11 wool blanket from The Cross
12 lace bedspread from Liberty
13 antique eiderdown from Tobias & the Angel

projects: *appliquéd matelasse bedspread:* fabric from Sanderson, striped ribbon from F. R. Street • *feather-stitched patchwork quilt:* antique remnants from Tobias & the Angel • *oak-leaf stenciled duvet:* fabric from Malabar Cotton Company • *velvet-edged bedspread:* fabric from F. R. Street, velvet piping from V. V. Rouleaux

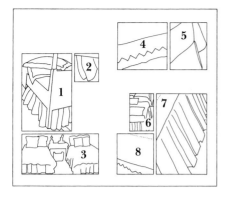

dust ruffles pages 48–49
1 organza fabric from McCulloch & Wallis, pillowcases from The Conran Shop
2 as above
3 blankets from The Conran Shop, dust ruffle fabric and pillows from Housemade
4 quilt from Tobias & the Angel, lace edging from Lunn Antiques, checked fabric from The Blue Door
5 fabric from Percheron
6 fabric from Housemade
7 as above
8 antique quilts and linens from Lunn Antiques

projects: *tailored pictorial print:* fabric from Christopher Moore Textiles • *soft green scallops:* fabric from Osborne & Little • *appliquéd zigzags:* plain fabric from Malabar Cotton Company, checked fabric from Designers Guild

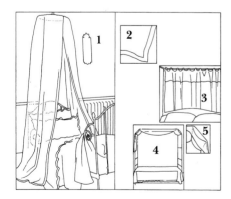

headboards pages 62–63
1 interior design by Reed Creative Services, all fabrics from Reed Creative Services
2 headboard from Simon Horn Furniture
3 headboard fabric from Colefax & Fowler
4 headboard fabric from F. R. Street
5 headboard fabric from Christopher Moore Textiles

projects: *florals and checks:* fabric from Cath Kidston, headboard made by Cover Up Designs of Kingsclere, pillowcase and pink blanket from Designers Guild • *tie-on padding:* fabric from Designers Guild • *hanging headboards:* plain fabrics from Osborne & Little, striped fabric from Malabar Cotton Company • *daisy motif headboard:* fabric from KA International, red upholstery nails from The Easy Chair, headboard made by Cover Up Designs of Kingsclere

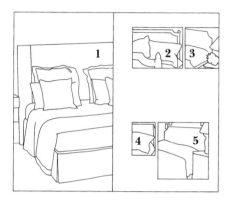

canopies pages 80–81
1 canopy from The Conran Shop, velvet ribbon from V. V. Rouleaux, sheets from The Monogrammed Linen Shop
2 as above
3 fabrics from John Lewis, bed from Shaker
4 fabric from Liberty, bed from Designers Guild
5 as above

projects: *scalloped corona:* checked fabric from Ian Mankin, dust ruffle fabric from Osborne & Little, corona from The Blue Door • *flowered voile bed canopy:* voile from Osborne & Little, lining from Designers Guild • *tied-on bed hangings:* fabric from Shaker • *striped scalloped canopy:* fabrics from Osborne & Little

page 98 antique textiles from Tobias & the Angel
page 106 antique quilt from Nicole Fabre, ticking from Malabar Cotton Company
page 110 fabric and pillows from Housemade, blankets from The Conran Shop
page 111 antique eiderdown from Tobias & the Angel
page 112 blanket from Tobias & the Angel, checked fabric from McKinney & Co
endpapers: antique bolster from Pimpernel & Partners

glossary

Appliqué
Applying a layer of fabric to a main fabric, usually with decorative stitching.

Batting
A thick soft padding material, made either from cotton or synthetic fibers, and used for upholstery and quilting.

Bias binding
A strip of cloth cut on the bias, at 45° to the selvage, which gives stretch to the fabric. Used as edging or to cover piping cord.

Bolster
A long, cylindrical pillow or cushion with flat ends.

Box pleat
A flat symmetrical pleat formed by folding the fabric to the back at each side of the pleat.

Braid
A woven ribbon used as edging or trimming.

Corona
A circular or semicircular structure mounted on the wall above a bed or sofa with draperies suspended from it.

Dust ruffle
A wide strip of fabric that runs around the base of a bed.

Flange
A flat rim or border that runs around a pillow or cushion.

Gingham
A plain-weave cotton cloth with a checked pattern.

Inverted pleat
A tailored pleat formed like a box pleat in reverse, so the edges of the pleat meet to conceal the additional fabric.

Linen
A strong and flexible fabric spun from the fibers of the flax plant.

Lining fabric
A secondary fabric used to back curtains, dust ruffles, bedspreads and other home furnishings to protect them from light and dust. Usually a cotton sateen fabric with a slight sheen.

Matelasse
A thick double cotton cloth, interlined at regular intervals to create a luxurious quilted effect.

Miter
The neat diagonal joining of two pieces of fabric where they meet at a corner.

Organza
A stiff, thin, sheer fabric.

Piping
A length of cord covered with bias binding and used as a decorative edging.

Piqué
A type of weave that produces a hard-wearing cloth with a ribbed texture and crisp finish.

Pleat
A sharp fold or crease, pressed or stitched in place.

Raw edge
The cut edge of fabric, without selvage or hem.

Scallops
A series of deep round curves used as a decorative edging.

Seam allowance
The narrow strip of raw-edged fabric left on each side of a stitched seam.

Selvage
The defined warp edge of the fabric, specially woven to prevent unraveling.

Sheers
Fine, translucent fabrics such as voile or organza that filter daylight and sunshine while preserving privacy.

Silk
A luxurious and soft yet strong fabric produced from a fiber spun by silkworms.

Stencil
A thin sheet of card or metal pierced with a simple pattern which is then brushed over with paint, leaving the pattern on the surface beneath the stencil.

Template
A shape cut from cardboard or paper and used to mark specific outlines on fabric.

Ticking
A closely woven, heavy cotton twill fabric with a fine stripe.

Toile de Jouy
A cotton cloth printed with pastoral scenes in a single color on a neutral background.

Velcro fastening
A double tape used for closing. One piece of tape is covered with a synthetic fuzz while the other is covered with tiny nylon fiber hooks. When pressed together, the two fabrics cling to each other until they are torn apart.

Velvet
A plush, luxurious warp-pile fabric with a short, closely woven pile. Can be made from cotton silk, or synthetic fibers.

Voile
A light plain-weave cotton or man-made fabric. Suitable for sheer curtains and bed drapes.

Warp
The threads woven across the length of fabric.

Weft
The threads woven across the width of fabric.

Width
The distance from selvage to selvage on any piece of fabric.

index

acknowledgements

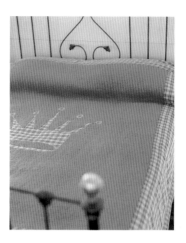

I owe a very big thank you to all the kind people who so generously gave
and loaned us fabric, beds, and bedding. These include The Blue Door,
Jane Churchill-Wish, Designers Guild, Pierre Frey, Cath Kidston, Liberty,
Malabar Cotton Co., Ian Mankin, Catherine Nimmo, Osborne & Little,
V. V. Rouleaux, Sanderson, and Shaker.
Many thanks to Tim Leese and Bobby Chance, Jonathan Reed, Liz Shirley,
Susie Tinsley, and Fiona Wheeler, all of whom kindly let us take
photographs in their homes – a very disruptive activity! This book
would not exist without Hänsi Schneider's exquisite sewing skills and
dedication – her work continues to be inspirational. To Helena Lynch –
who also made many items for photography, often in haste but
always perfect – thank you.
James Merrell's photographs and complete understanding of the subject
are the essence of professionalism. Lizzie Sander's illustrations are works of
art that bring the sewing projects to life. Both are greatly appreciated.
The Ryland Peters & Small team continue to produce
books of the highest caliber – congratulations.
Finally, to Janey Joicey-Cecil and Catherine Coombes, who have
done so much of the hard work, both on photo shoots and at home,
thank you both for your help.

dedication

For Carol and Mark Glasser, with everlasting friendship and love.